Every Kid's Guide to
Handling Illness

Written by

JOY BERRY

GROLIER ENTERPRISES INC.
Danbury, Connecticut

About the Author and Publisher

Joy Berry's mission in life is to help families cope with everyday problems and to help children become competent, responsible, happy individuals. To achieve her goal, she has written over two hundred self-help books for children from infancy through age twelve. Her work has revolutionized children's publishing by providing families with practical, how-to, living skills information that was previously unavailable in children's books.

Joy has gathered a dedicated team of experts, including psychologists, educators, child developmentalists, writers, editors, designers, and artists to form her publishing company and to help produce her work.

The company, Living Skills Press, produces thoroughly researched books and audiovisual materials that successfully combine humor and education to teach children subjects ranging from how to clean a bedroom to how to resolve problems and get along with other people.

Managing Editor: Ellen Klarberg
Copy Editors: Annette Gooch
Contributing Editors: Libby Byers, Patricia Dryer, M.D., Yona Flemming,
Dan Gurney, James Gough, M.D., Roger Pitzen, M.D., Gretchen Savidge
Editorial Assistant: Lana Eberhard

Art Director: Jennifer Wiezel
Designer: Laurie Westdahl, Jennifer Wiezel
Illustration Designer: Bartholomew
Inking Artist: Dave Hanney
Coloring Artist: Linda Hanney
Lettering Artist: Linda Hanney
Production Artist: Gail Miller

Typographer: Communication Graphics

A physical illness can interfere with your body's ability to do the wonderful things it can ordinarily do.

In **Every Kid's Guide to Handling Illness,** you will learn about
- physical illnesses,
- relief from general symptoms,
- relief from specific symptoms, and
- ways to avoid physical illnesses.

A **physical illness** is an unhealthy condition of the body.

Some physical illnesses develop when certain kinds of living organisms **(germs)** enter the body. Illnesses caused by germs are called **infectious diseases.**

Some physical illnesses occur when certain kinds of non-living substances **(allergens)** enter the body.

Illnesses caused by allergens are called **allergic diseases.**

Infectious and allergic diseases can cause pain and discomfort or even cause your body to respond in unusual ways.

The unusual functions, feelings of discomfort, and pain you experience as a result of disease are called **disease symptoms.**

Some symptoms are common to almost all illnesses.
These are called **general symptoms.**

Some symptoms occur only with certain illnesses.
These are called **specific symptoms.**

Symptoms can serve a useful purpose. They can
- let you know that harmful germs or allergens have invaded your body and
- help your body get rid of those harmful germs or allergens.

There are things you can do to make yourself more comfortable while your body does what it needs to do to get rid of the germs or allergens that are threatening its well-being.

Making yourself more comfortable during an illness is called **relieving the symptoms.**

Things to do for a *fever* (a body temperature higher than approximately 100°):

- Wet a washcloth with lukewarm water. Rub the washcloth all over your body. Then allow your body to air dry.
- Massage your body while you take a lukewarm shower. Allow your body to air dry.

See a doctor if your fever lasts for more than a day or two. Your doctor might recommend using a medication to help reduce your fever.

Things to do for *chills:*
- Get in a warm, comfortable environment.
- Wrap yourself loosely in a blanket.
- Drink a warm beverage.

See your doctor if your chills persist.

Things to do for unusual *tiredness:*
- Avoid vigorous physical activity.
- Get comfortable.
- Allow your body to rest.

Things to do for **body aches:**

■ Take a warm bath or shower.
■ Apply a heating pad or hot water bottle to the painful area.
■ Get comfortable.
■ Allow your muscles to relax.

See a doctor if your body aches persist. Your doctor might recommend using a medication to relieve the pain.

Things to do for a **headache:**
- Avoid bright lights.
- Lie down in a darkened room.
- Try to sleep.

Gently massaging or applying a cool, damp cloth to the painful area sometimes helps. See a doctor if your headache persists. Your doctor might recommend using a medication to relieve the pain.

Things to do for *neck stiffness and pain:*

■ Avoid moving your neck.
■ Apply a heating pad or hot water bottle to the painful area.

See your doctor immediately if you also have severe vomiting or a fever higher than 103°F.

Things to do for *irritated eyes:*
- Avoid rubbing your eyes.
- Splash cool water into your eyes.
- Close your eyes and cover them with a cool, wet washcloth.

See a doctor if your irritation persists or if pain develops. Your doctor might recommend gently flooding your eyes with a saline solution or using antibiotic eyedrops.

Things to do for an *earache:*

■ Avoid putting anything into your ear.

■ Do not move your head around any more than is necessary.

■ Hold a heating pad or hot water bottle over the affected ear.

See a doctor if there is any discharge from your ear or if the pain persists. Your doctor might recommend using a nasal spray or an antibiotic medication.

Things to do for a *sore throat:*

- Drink plenty of fluids.
- Gargle with a solution consisting of 1/2 teaspoon of salt dissolved in 1 cup of water.
- Gargle with regular tea.
- Use sugar-free menthol lozenges.
- Drink warm tea flavored with honey or lemon.

See a doctor if your sore throat persists. Your doctor might recommend using a throat spray or an antibiotic medication.

Things to do for *hoarseness:*

- Use your voice as little as possible.
- Breathe in the steam from a vaporizer or hot shower or bath.
- Drink warm tea flavored with honey or lemon.

Things to do for *canker sores:*

■ Dry the sore with a cotton swab and apply a special solution that is available from your pharmacist.

■ Take a lysine supplement in an amount recommended by your doctor.

See a doctor if your canker sores persist. Your doctor might recommend adding a zinc supplement to your diet.

Things to do for **cold sores** (fever blisters):
■ Avoid touching or picking at the sore.
■ Apply a special solution that is available from your
   pharmacist.

See a doctor if your cold sores persist. Your
doctor might recommend adding a lysine supplement
to your diet.

Things to do for a **stuffy nose:**
- Drink plenty of fluids.
- Breathe in the steam from a vaporizer or hot shower or bath.
- Rub a menthol salve inside your nostrils.

See your doctor if your nasal congestion persists. Your doctor might recommend using a saline nasal spray or decongestant. Any nasal spray should be used for a short time only.

Things to do for a ***runny nose:***

- Gently blow your nose into a soft tissue.
- Discard the tissue immediately after use.
- Avoid rubbing your nose and the area around it.
- Rinse your nasal passages with salt water. Your parents or a doctor or nurse can show you how to do this.

See a doctor if your nasal discharge is a yellow or green color. Your doctor might recommend using an antibiotic or a decongestant medication.

Things to do for *coughing:*

■ Drink plenty of fluids.

■ Drink chicken broth.

■ Use sugar-free peppermint drops.

■ Breathe in steam from a vaporizer or hot shower or bath.

See a doctor if your cough persists. Your doctor might recommend using an expectorant, a decongestant, or an antibiotic medication.

Things to do for **wheezing:**
- Drink plenty of fluids, especially warm tea.
- Breathe in steam from a vaporizer or hot shower or bath.

See a doctor if your wheezing persists. Your doctor might recommend using a bronchodilator or an antibiotic medication.

Things to do for **diarrhea:**

■ Avoid eating fruit (except bananas and applesauce).

■ Avoid drinking fruit juices and eating dairy products.

See your doctor if your diarrhea persists. Your doctor might recommend using an anti-diarrheal or antibiotic medication.

Things to do for *constipation:*

- Drink plenty of fluids (especially fruit juices such as prune or apple juice).
- Eat food that contains fiber (such as fruit, vegetables, and whole grains).
- Get plenty of exercise.

See your doctor if your constipation persists. Your doctor might recommend using mineral oil, milk of magnesia, or some other mild laxative.

Things to do for **nausea:**

■ Avoid eating (especially dairy products and solid foods).

■ Suck on small pieces of crushed ice.

■ Slowly sip a carbonated beverage. Allow the bubbles to disappear first.

Things to do for *vomiting:*

- Avoid eating immediately after vomiting (especially avoid eating dairy products and solid foods).
- After 30 minutes or an hour, suck on small pieces of crushed ice or slowly sip a carbonated beverage. Allow the bubbles to disappear first.
- When your appetite returns, drink chicken broth.
- Several hours after you have drunk some chicken broth, you might want to eat hot cereal or applesauce.

See a doctor if your vomiting persists. Your doctor might recommend using a suppository or some other medication to help you stop vomiting.

Things to do for a **stomach ache:**

Observe how you feel:

- Exactly where is the pain?
- Is the pain sharp, dull, burning, or aching?
- Is the pain steady or does it come and go?
- Does eating have any effect on the pain?
- Do you have any other symptoms (for example, vomiting and diarrhea)?

Relate your observations to a doctor. The doctor might want to examine you.

Whenever you have a stomach ache, you need to
- avoid eating solid foods,
- avoid drinking anything, and
- avoid taking laxatives or pain medications unless a doctor recommends them.

Things to do for *problems with urinating:*
Let your doctor know immediately if

■ you have blood in your urine,
■ your urine is cloudy or discolored,
■ you feel burning or pain whenever you urinate, or
■ you are urinating much more frequently than usual.

Your doctor might want to examine you or might recommend drinking cranberry juice or using an antibiotic medication.

Things to do for *skin rashes:*
- Avoid scratching the affected area.
- Keep the area clean and dry.

See a doctor if the rash persists or spreads. Your doctor might recommend using a lotion, cream, or oral medication.

Never use medication unless you have your parent's permission to do so.

Always follow the doctor's instructions for using medication that he or she has prescribed.

A healthy body is less likely to be affected by germs and allergens. There are things you can do to keep your body healthy.

Eat the right foods

Eat the following foods every day:

- 2 fruits (one should be a citrus fruit)
- 2 vegetables (one should be a dark green or deep yellow)
- 2 or more servings of fish, poultry, dried beans, dried peas, lentils, or lowfat cottage cheese
- 4 or more servings of whole-grain, enriched, or restored bread or cereal
- 2 or more cups of nonfat milk

Avoid eating too much of these foods:

- red meat
- sugar
- salt
- fat

Drink plenty of water.
Drink several glasses of water every day.

Get plenty of fresh air and sunshine.
Work and play outside in the fresh air and sunshine as often as possible. Be sure to use a sunscreen if there is a chance you could get sunburned.

Get plenty of exercise.

Do activities that require you to use your body's large muscles at least 30 minutes every day.

Get enough rest.

Take time during the day to rest your body by sitting or lying down.

Sleep at least eight to ten hours every night.

Keep your body clean.
- Wash your entire body every day.
- Shampoo your hair regularly.
- Wash your hands before you eat.
- Brush and floss your teeth after eating.

Besides keeping your body healthy, there are other things you can do to avoid illness. You can avoid infectious diseases by staying away from
- people who have infectious diseases,
- polluted water, and
- contaminated food.

You can also avoid some infectious diseases by receiving appropriate immunizations.

Children are often immunized for these diseases:
- diphtheria
- whooping cough
- tetanus
- polio
- mumps
- measles
- German measles
- hemophilus influenza

You can avoid allergic diseases by staying away from allergens that your body cannot tolerate. This might include things such as these:

- dust
- pollens from grasses, trees, and weeds
- certain foods
- animal hair

You can also avoid some allergic diseases by receiving injections that help your body develop a tolerance for certain allergens.

A doctor can be a key person in helping you
- avoid physical illnesses and
- recover from physical illnesses.

To maintain good health, you should see a doctor
- approximately once a year for a general check-up and
- whenever you are having a difficult time recovering from an illness.

Keeping your body healthy and knowing what to do when you have an illness can help you do the things you need to do to be well and happy.